Look Out Animal

by Noah Burton

Look Out Animal ©2018 by **Noah Burton**. Published in the United States by Vegetarian Alcoholic Press. Not one part of this work may be reproduced without expressed written consent from the author. For more information, please contact vegalpress@gmail.com

Cover Art: Patrick Yagow
Design: Ryan Harrison

for my folks

Table of Contents

Anger for the Earth.....1
Where the trees open up at the city limits.....2
Clay County, Kansas.....3
Desire.....4
The Springfield Business.....5
Rotate and we are a World.....6
When They Found Me, I Couldn't Speak Their Language.....7
Mobius Strip.....8
Light Light Always Light.....9
Earthboy.....10
Almanac.....11
Ten years after the Roswell Invasion.....13
Turning.....14
Two Poems for Russell Edson.....16
Offerings.....17
Outside the inner circle there's a larger circle.....18
Macrostitches.....19
Paths.....20
Tax Season.....21
With the Razz of The Garden.....22
Welcome Party.....23
Wabi-Sabi.....24
It is the last day of January.....25
Snow Set.....26
I Mixed Up the Goats.....27
Companions.....28
Span of Time.....29
The Book is Not life.....30
Anti-matter.....31
Olive.....32

The Blind Knife.....33

Spot.....34

Days of Robert The Food Processor.....36

The Buzz Pear.....37

B-Theater.....38

Chance to This.....39

Indra's Net.....40

Erik Satie The Phonometrician.....42

Feelings are Pointless.....43

Unfog.....44

Consciousness is a Universal Feature of All Things.....46

Face Poem.....47

Spirit and Philosophy.....48

Muad'Dib.....49

Finders....50

Mother.....51

No one ever fails in a universe of tables.....52

All God's Children in the Laboratory.....53

Anger for the Earth

Green in the old mascara
on your eyes and on the pale
pears. As close as I get
we are apart. There is a rhino
in me: it walks. There is
a chimpanzee in you: it throws.
There is nothing that does not
grow on us. Over the field,
the stalks blow. We are standing
near a vined chimney
while night washes itself
with a damp clock.

Where the trees open up at the city limits.

"Carry on," he says, chewing
        a plum, "carry on
over that dam.
                Go ahead.
        Just balance those
bags of feed
                on your shoulders."

                "But, I didn't ask for this.
I just wanted to visit
        the town over.
                I'd heard there's
a lovely theater there where
all the magicians are
                penguins making each other
disappear right on stage for
        one night only."

"You heard right.
            There's also a horse
and he's hungry."

Clay County, Kansas

The shadows of the silos and the shadows
of the wheat are more than the moon
could ask for during her photo shoot.
Her lens is as round as Kansas is rectangular,
but just as empty and desolate as geometry.
In moonlight, the silos stand like priests
waiting for the end of the world to speak.
The tornado touches down.
Engines fly out of the plains.
The priests fly out of the plains.
Again, wind. A bent weathervane
scraps itself like a broken oboe reed.
So long, clouds. Hello, moon.

Desire

The smallest window of the gem
held in the monkey's hand
glimmers with carnival lights.
Good news! Life's a cartoon
in which our hands keep getting larger
and larger, wanting more as we walk
into the next panel. The cross-hatched city
looms over us until our issues are up,
our lives are rare, left in a musty box
in the comic book store on Broad Street.
Good news, in the middle of my life,
they remade me. My hands smaller.
My muscles a bit more defined, but I lost
my smart, weak, and clumsy sidekick.
They've taken away some color from my cape.

The Springfield Business

The fire tower's hornet's nest collapsing. After the siege,
the town of Springfield calls it a defensive victory—
"We win!" says the Mayor over the town megaphones, "Now
we can stop this silly notion that one lot of us is better
than the other." The crowd from Fairfax slumps, dragging
their Converses, pulling their pup-tents. But tomorrow, this time,
the homes on Decatur will be lit up—I mean really blazing—sooty feet
running out of front stoops, kitchen windows throwing flames like
kitchen pots. The crowd back in Springfield, a Fairfax mob now—
"If you don't give us another one of your streets, know what!?"
one member, Ms. Beale, a rooster keeper, says, "We'll burn it! Then
we'll burn the next one! And the next one!"—"Heaven's no!" says Mr. Coppola,
the Fairfax Horologist, "Where would we sleep after we finished
with all this Springfield business?" The mob arguing with
itself like a pinball machine, while, hurtling down Maritime Lane,
a group of fire fighters toss off burning mattresses,
springed coils boinging on the sidewalk past the post office.

Rotate and we are a World

Tree branches—
algae waves—above the rapids,
fresh grass and
Sure, I say,
and go with you,
to the garden, and we look
at the bamboo fence,
but through the reeds I
at you as an ox-cart
rolls by.
      This is new,
this particular world—
the mill, and fence, and us,
old and new How do we
want to see it,
the lit archipelago
bringing us here by
merely checking
the sturdiness of a fence
in a garden, here, in love,
between our faces
with afternoon light and
an ox-cart pulling manure,
shaking lavender flowers.

When They Found Me, I Couldn't Speak Their Language

All the toasters chewing
the bread. The sink
going down the drain.
I'm at the mirror to see
if there's anything in my teeth—
a black bean, a tear of mint.
The front door creaks open.
It's my bike again, taking my wallet,
slipping out, rocking the stairs
like a giddy-up horsey.
He'll be back. I'm out of soap.
We've discussed this.
But, the corner store
doesn't serve bikes.

Mobius Strip

Everything's occurred, but
there's only one example of it.
At most it's this cheetah, outside
the coastal village's arcade,
that's been flashing me—but no one
has ever caught it on film, so
no one believes me, or
the copper singularity in its stripes.
Jerry, coming over,
takes another dollar
from my pocket. He's like
a ski-ball score, running up all day.
Tim leaves at noon,
yelling about his terrible weekend—
he moved some beds,
pocketed a piece of jewelry,
white out on the side-road,
hit a fucking cow
Then he lost at Dig Dug.
There's only one example of
everything—it's Dig Dug.
Outside, slipping sideways
into the thin paw tracks
on the beach, I stand up
waving at that cheetah
getting pummeled by a wave.

Light Light Always Light

after Aaron Gerber

death by Google death by chocolate Bye-Bye's death by grass death by Orrtanna, PA death
by M.I.A. death by Defjam records death by Brian McKnight death by the Man of Steel

flying in with death by the death cape death by leeches death by beaches death by sneezes
death by a pile of teddy bears death by elephant spit death by the Sex Pistols loading death

on a death screen death by brother death by sister death by Stephen King and Thich Nhat Hanh
in collaboration with Andy Warhol on the eve of the death of the reel to reel by laser disc death

by rainbows ohhh!!! death by rainbows by rainbows by rainbows by by rainbows by by rainbows
by a rainbow by a rainbow by a rainbow and rainbow and rainbow and rainbow and rainbow…

Earthboy

A rod in his hands
for digging in the garden.
Crawling in. The hole
closing above him.
Artichokes rooting.
Ginger. Like a pillow
behind his head—a potato.
The vegetables form a tribunal.
Decide that he can
stay here, and will.

Almanac

    "Well, that about does it," Ralph's hands
   clapping together like a
     pizza pie maker's.
        The last barrow
dumped in the mill.

     Then the other grain pusher
standing up, straightening out
   his back, cracks it.

        "Does what?"

   The windmill turns, slicing up
     the moon. Impenetrable.
  Impenetrable.

"All the grain's gone" says Ralph.

       "Where to?"

"Into the mill
    of course."
      "What about the wind?"

"What wind?

      "That wind."

    The tornado stands up.

 "Ah yes, right on time. Here," says Ralph

"take these
 ankle weights."

Ten years after the Roswell invasion

Sore from stuffing people
into these flimsy manilla folders.
The isles, quite cramped.
Sucking in my gut. Yup—
not any younger. But,
not a chance to put in
my two weeks. All hours.
Fingers ringing the bell,
fiddling with pens and
forms and shirt sleeves.
The line to my desk
going around the block.
Everyone getting limber.
Stretching like falling dominos.

Turning

I cut the lights
and pull the quilt
up over me.
But first,

I should tell you
the car is
in neutral
and twisting
down the road

through the apple orchard
at midnight.
The radio off.

The fruit dropping.
Running along
beside my hatchback,
deer feet fall
like satellites
in a desert.
I wonder how
this will end.
When will the
deer fan out
into the rows?
You could be anywhere
at midnight
and realize *well...*

so what? The engine,
completely silent.
The wind, whipping
the fence posts—You,
at the window

of your tiny kitchen,
watching deer
turning into trees.

Two Poems for Russell Edson

I.

Before the old poet died,
I had planned on writing him.
Russell, does this work for you?
I ask him. *No, Noah, this really
doesn't work for me. Alrighty,*
I say to him. *Wait, maybe
we'll do something here,* he says,
*write down the word 'cannon'
and flip me over and rub
my eraser head on that word
like a match on the side of a stone
face. I'll make that graphite
smudge like smoke—you'll call me
The Cannon Man, and I'll call you
Gunpowder Burton.*

II.

Russell Edson, *Yes, Noah Boah?*
Can we make a house together?
Sure. And it shall be made of snow.
But then it'll melt in the summer.
Thank God, I'm thirsty, aren't you?

Offerings

Boys always with ladders
coming to pick
apples that grew out
of your crooked arms,
blushing women
appearing like sunset
in windows. Early fall.
For you it was
delightful then
until you thought
of something else.
You'd let the apples fall
overnight. The next day
broke out with a fruit fight.
Skin breaking all over.
Tears. Stumbles.
Legs dragged
through the rows.
People take things
the wrong way, so often.

Outside the inner circle there's a larger circle
Outside the larger circle there's a tree
Outside the tree there's a pond

Let's move it two feet

to the left, one boulder mover

says to the other.

Why not two feet to the right?

says the other.

Well damn it, Monica,

cries the first boulder mover,

there's a tree there.

Macrostitches

Unusual Trade Function
Wild ice.

Your Breath
Secret changing interior.

Earth is Awake
Boats sailing.

Pocket Airplanes
Flies lack silliness.

The Perfect Setting
A coat.

Diamond Drops
Under a sprinkler.

Our Radio Towers
Moon eraser.

Two Thumbs
Cracked kitchen plate.

The Big World
Small people.

Paths

Some nights God takes off his watch,
puts it on his dresser, thinking,
I need a drink. Throws his tie
on the back of the chair,
and hits up the mini-bar.
A couple in their room
jumps from one bed to the other.
The meteor shower, crossing
the windows. In the lobby,
someone looks at him,
walks up, says *hello*.
Other nights, he just goes to bed
with that watch still on his wrist.

Tax Season

It scrolls down the screen
to the next page and there's
a box to check whether
you're filing taxes for yourself, or
for someone else, or someone who died.
So, Zach, someone must be doing this
this season for you,
all the lights are on in their den
and the computer is on
and your name is typed in the HR block website.
But in York, Maine the arcade
opens at 7pm,
the ski-ball machines firing up,
getting loaded, the quarters
dropping into the slots,
the tickets coming out, and
just off work we look like mimes
in our striped chef pants.

With the Razz of The Garden

How say you pain?
Pleasureless pain,
a rambling flower
making a funny
to a chive plant? The ginger
wrapped in the dirt
is a tetherball. A splay of mud
is on a work glove in
a wheel barrow
Inside, the house organ
rattles another bar off
in the dining room dusk—
Is that maple?
No, this is oak. It plays
like maple. Well,
a bone's a bone.
Wood is wood.
Healing is painful,
a square garden we pick at
and tend to— the deer
walk away at night
with flowers in their mouths
and there's a light from
a nearby train—

Welcome Party

It's raining
      black cherries,
           heavy drops,
     outside the town gate.
In front of the guardian, on a horse
        galloping up,

                      "I'm sorry," Connie says. "I dropped
                          my I.D Card."

"You may not enter," says the guardian.

        "Don't you see it's raining out
              my clothes are getting wet, the sky
     is open, so why not open your gate?"

"Oh. That's what all this is."
                  his stone hand,
      palm out, plop drops.

               "Please. My horse is soaked."

"No he's not. He's just shrinking."

         Connie's eyes looking down, legs touching
                the ground, the horse
    looks up,
        a tiny neigh,
a pony thing.

Wabi-Sabi

Technically, you're doing a poor job. You have no form.
Your hatchet flails down into the uprooted stump.
The beagle howls. George Williams, Mr. Horton, Hilliary,
and the other neighbors spring up in their beds.
The dog's mug and paws clatter the chain-link fence
like an ambitious kid assigned to the chimes in music class
sweeping the tiny stick over the metal bars
in gloriously abrupt, halted, and sped up glissandos
that out perform the glockenspiels and make the triangle feel
even more alone and pointless.

Despite the fact that everyone you saw yesterday seemed
so much happier than you, don't you feel a bit better right now?
Your work may achieve what the Roshis speak of:
Wabi-sabi in the stump. Perfection in imperfection—
gashes si-goggly like fallen trees in a forest
or the green of moss glowing on anything when it's grey out,
or the hatchet tilted in the corner of your living room
and your decision to take a night off of listening to Stereolab
on opium, and going out back to shave,
whittle, chop, and cut at a piece of hickory.
The neighbors' kitchen lights flick on,
visored faces against the windows.

It is the last day of January

the equator of calendar orchards
between the fat dark hinges
of last year and this year
is January, pulsing into
star light—traveling away,
the snow banks not melting,
the Explorers always covered in salt,
no one—not you or the sled
you slid in on—knows
what will happen next,
after work, after January.
No one is planning. No one is moving.
No one is waving goodbye,
or hello, snow drifts
blowing about, equal
parts beginning and end.

Snow Set

Make us up a field of bright flakes
dimming as night presses
and the sun says, *forget this*,
and leaves us. There's a green barn
someplace in Kansas not on fire.
The radiator is saying, *the pipes
are playing drums*. We're all stoned
and no one is paranoid. The town too
isn't on fire, with a crowd
of blessed sneezers singing oh
holy night for the Indiglow
circle of light, the town clock
glowing against burnt wheat.

I Mixed Up the Goats

One's name is Sophie,
the brown one,
the other's name is Agnes,
the black one, and their names
suit them. What with
Sophie being the younger
looking of the two, though both
are well past sixteen years
(which is mostly like sheep years
but with shorter pelts).
Agnes, the brown one,
is the older of the two
with two full horns and one short one,
her brown coat and plump udders
blow in the short field wind with the hay.
Sophie gets mad at Agnes,
she's the alpha goat, Agnes is
in her brown coat and Sophie,
the black one, is a brown goat
that looks younger than the older,
Agnes. Suddenly, the chicken
walks out of the barn, named Sunshine,
but I like to call her Chicken.

Companions

To get the compass
back you just need
to stick your hand
into your
pocket. The map,
on the other hand—
I'm not sure where
you put that.

Span of Time

Go on once

you get there.

What's there? Hell,

there's probably a

hill under an old

source of light

and we're looking

up at it and it's

looking down at us

and an astronomer

is saying, "You are

not alive anymore, star"

and the star is saying,

"So are you."

The Book Is Not Life

No one,
standing around
Grandma's bed, her last
breath lifting,
turned around,
shut the door, said,
"Wow, what a good life!"
Though it was.

Anti-matter

Everything I ever say
begins and ends nearly the same way—
toast in a kenmore toaster.

Olive

The oil drop on the floor
dropped from your hand
and there is a world
there inside it where
you are big-faced,
a small ceiling fan
above you, the dome
of the room and
another world
in your palm with
inlets and roads,
creased grounding,
clenched as you yell
fuck over a dropped
world and another
and another

The Blind Knife

Leaving his studio apartment, Benny
gets his blade tip stuck in the door frame.
Cuts people in line at the corner store.
Earlier he clanged his stainless head
on a coat rack—the down feathers flew.
This always happens. A bigger problem
with Benny—helping and hurting—
falling over onto a wedding cake,
everyone cheers! Lopping off
a head, everyone screams! When
he arrives at the birthday, he slashes
the piñata open. Party whistles
fizzle out on the porch, dropping
mouths of parents and children,
the Tiki torch lights flickering. Then
"Candy!" everyone yells, "You did it,
Benny! You did it!" Sundresses and
overalls stain with melted Zero bars
and Jolly Ranchers. Over on a stump,
the boy with the bat and blindfold
sighs, *This always happens.*

Spot

The Sauer's
Vanilla neon sign
lighting
      up on the corner
of Meadow and Broad one
tube at a time
          the 'S' and
          'A' and 'U' 'E'
'R' filling with the glowing
extractor's tub of
fluorescent vanilla
white and red and it
        smells sweet
     around here. A flashing
Your kick-flip caught
over the bus bench
caught in the tiny bright
SLR camera screen I'm
using again tonight,
        years later,
with the same
kind of
    light
coming down
on the corner of
Central and Main from
Jeremy's Pizza sign
        and bouncing
     off a panicle of a
purple hydrangea—a flashing
over the camera's

lens—how sweet
it smells here too.

Days of Robert The Food Processor

Low to the ground, under
the table, Robert never
gets dizzy. Not plugged in.
Not spinning, grinding up
walnuts or blending a root.
His red round button unclicked,
bladed brow arch unquivered.
Then a hand grabs on to his
chord, slips it into the wall socket.
A timer ringing over the oven.
Robert's vertigo kicking in
in the emulsification of
an olive oil based salad dressing.
Nauseous. A golden sea
in his head, whirling.

The Buzz Pear

Limb, admit it
        that you are a tree.

        Head, I will
when you say you
        are a body.

Body, I will not
        until you give me a
                proper perch.

Neck,
you're a nest,
        can't you see that?

Brains, oh,
        a pink walnut.

B-Theater

Do you believe in the man who hung the moon?
How about that one who's turning the time machine on?
Have you any faith in the projector's bulb?
How about the projectionist? Have you heard
of his secret desire to become a Peachleaf Willow?
Have you ever wanted to be a Peachleaf Willow
so you could hang up the moon? But trees grow
that tall just in the movies, right?
Are those empty seats staring at us?
The movie, is it playing? Are you trying
to watch the time machine warp into
the next scene? When will it get there?
If you don't think I can finish all this licorice
by myself, why not help me?

Chance to This

Flip this coin and, either way,
I'm telling you why I've decided
to become an excavator of horses—
their bodies impeccably intact
like stone ships left sunk
in the mercury waters of Europa:
I've had enough of our world.
Dearest dear dear and dear,
to you I toss my socks.
I've dug for a while now
so the water doesn't smell
like the volcano we watch
late at night together, a shower
of earth borne stars falling off
a brightening back side.

Indra's Net

Outside the smoking shack
    by the stacked triangle
  cord of wood, the carpenter
untangles a knot

"This thing won't give!"

     His brother, Ben, the trapper, drops
  the deer's hind legs
    onto the porch, says

        "Like mother use to say,
   'One leaves the carriage and walks,'
 course sometimes the door is locked,
    the horses, angsty, rearing up,
        running off,
  then you find yourself stuck,
rolling down the path,
   lamp fixtures
     rocking between the bench,
       like that knot you're shaking at"

    The carpenter slams.
  Thunder stirring behind the
   mountain like a war
whoop booming, booming

     "Come on now," Ben says,
  "hitting it on the porch won't help."

        Wood creaks and cool
    breathe from nostrils rising, antlers
                            smacking the pillars.

        "You've woke the deer."

Erik Satie The Phonometrician

You've called me a parlor composer.
Well, if I am, to you, so basic,
then allow me, instead, a ruler
and the arithmetic of school children.
Critique me only on my ability to measure
how close the woman is as you stand at her doorway—
her hands pulling the chopsticks from her oriental bun,
dropped hands and wood on the comforter sheet.
The oak floor creaks. The lamp shade wobbles
near the window by the bed.
Street cars muffling with snow
As a piano lesson finishes,
her gown slips over the dimple on her lower back.

Feelings are Pointless

Walking up to the top of Mount Takao,
looking down, seeing the jagged switchback,
a grey white anxious topography, and
today, closing the pickle jar, he broke
the glass, sour in his hand, and
the shards cut him. Yet, I feel
my flesh is a small path on the small
mountain where the first loom was crafted
and shawls woven to cover swords
that beam as the weaver watches
the sun and day and says, *You—*
you are pointless, Day, and the day
turns darkly from the peak
to the night, and the swords, covered
with the shawls, hide their points.

Unfog

A late happiness for the past
comes in with the light
beam glazing over coconut
and blueberry pastries in
Country Style Donuts. I flew here
remembering a girl I once
lived with, a parked car
we once sat in, her head
on my shoulder, the drive-in
playing *The Dark Knight*, tuning
the radio to the right station,
having to open the windows
to unfog the windows and it's
hot in here, the mosquitos come in,
they come in single file like
a factory then expand out
like a factory drilling us—
so much bores me now
Hippy hugs. My new age.
This polished tiger's eye
energizing my aura.
Once there were many
tomato plants in a garden,
oh then, with the mint,
I was full—I think it was
last night I dreamed of you,
Meesagh and Meeahd
and Omid telling me
the motorcyclist swerved
your mother into the truck's engine.

We sat there. With rice and kabob.
The Tysons Corner shoppers,
leaving for the night. The late night
movie goers going in
the cineplex, light reel fanning
over the screen, flashed hairdos:
your father swimming, his friend
in Iranian seawater, a shark bite
and dying in the car—"but
that's how things go," he'd say,
"if they died, they died."
A velvet mountain in the dream
like the red velvet chairs of
the movie theaters, the chairs
after the memorial service, pushed out
like this death, or that death,
like fall maple leaves caught.

Consciousness is a Universal Feature of All Things

Partly because the sky is blue
the squirrel is, itself, sad:
the tents with their
motionless flags and fire flames
in the spice colored wind.
Carrying leather luggage,
the young horse with the dead samurai
in the Smithsonian display scene
sits on a crinkled leaf.
The girl swings her sister's folded
umbrella: "Jean, Jean, why does he
have a flute *and* a sword?" Funny
thing solitude is—a village of small buckets,
overflowing plastic rain.

Face Poem

The eyes open and the hand
moves up to the mouth
over the desk in the
office of the endless
other faces that are all
watching the clock move
closer to 5 o'clock
getting slower as
it gets closer—all things
slow down before
reaching a destination.
Standing up, this poem
follows the other poems out.
This poem doesn't have to clock out,
it's on salary. But,
it does need a new face.
It's unsure where its nose is,
how to smell or think,
with its flat brain folded into
the pocket of a taxi cab seat.

Spirit and Philosophy

Some light behind you
in the tree line and between
the night clouds—you, my
dim reflection! How
like me to look at you.
Behind me is the wall.
Behind you is the forest.
In front of us both is
the window. You can get up
and walk back into the dark
green and build a fire
with shadow wood if
you want, chop at it,
hurl it up the pile, burning
white sage and mantra papers.
You can even get
more naked than you are
already, and roast a pig.
But I'll stand up. Stub my toe,
hit the drying rack, crashing,
cry out, *piece of shit!*
The neighbor's dog barking,
but there's ritual in that too.

Muad'Dib

Every time, walking,
we see a wall in the woods
it's as if it wasn't built but
emerged, cracking roots,
lifting dirt and mica
like the sand worms of Dune in
the spiced desert of Arrakis
and that's why I'm telling you
let's ride this thing. Hoist your
leg up and over. *But it won't
take us anywhere.* That's
what you say now but look:
a mushroom grew last night,
latched on, riding the wall
and moonlight and moss,
and by doing so it traveled
terrains without really
moving anywhere at all—
on the back of a stone worm.
Maples falling and fiddle heads
curl, and perhaps I'll
have a beard someday
perhaps your hair will gray,
it's better than having
a short wall between us while
taking a Tuesday afternoon
stroll in a bird watching park.

Finders

The stone
in your hand,
where'd you get it?
Never mind.
Doesn't matter.
Don't ever
put it down.

Mother

We're never entirely old—
just as we're never entirely the same
person as a minute ago
walking over the foot bridge
to the point, a state
park, collecting winter
berry branches in bundles
for the vase in my kitchen.
A rower, gliding by, waves at us,
and I wave back before we
turn into the tree line and
he rows out of the inlet.
We're both here on this Earth
though it is never entirely
the same for the both of us—
except now I'm older
and you're older too.

"no one ever fails in a universe of tables"

no one ever fails in a universe of tables
where nothing ever falls off
without falling on another table
so we hold everything and everything's
held by us and we are held by all of it
so we never fail to keep a table top ready
to hold whatever else may come
then I'd gather we'd expect it
to be another table but here we are
propped up cleared and all standing
surprised together that it's a table

All God's Children in the Laboratory

I told you about the replicator
I told you about the replicator
I told you about the replicator

yes yes I know I know
yes yes I know I know
I said watch out I said

watch out I said yes
yes I know I know
you warned me

because you care
about me you warned me
because you care about me

no I don't care I love no
I don't care I love and
so do I and so do I

I'm grateful for the following publications that have published versions of the poems in this collection:

"Rotate and We Are a World", *Paperbag, Issue No. 9,* "Light Light Always Light", *Metatron Press' Omega Blog,* "Two Poems for Russell Edson", "Outside the inner circle there's a larger circle...", *fog machine,* "Macrostitches", *Cruel Garters,* "Turning", *Grasslimb,* "no one ever fails in a universe of tables", "Finders", *Outlook Springs,* "Snow Set", "When They Found Me I Couldn't Speak Their Language", "Mobius Strip", *gobbet,* "Anger for the Earth", *Dirty Chai,* "Earthboy", *The Doctor T.J. Eckleburg Review,* "Companions", *Kenning Journal,* "Tax Season", "Feelings are Pointless", *Baldhip magazine,* "Wabi-Sabi", *Burningword*

I am endlessly thankful for the following harbingers of light and inspiration without whom this book would not be made:

Aaron Gerber, Caro Clark, Chris Messinger, Doug Fuller, Kathleen Graber, David Wojahn, Claire Donato, Danniel Schoonebeek, Tanya Larkin, Charles Simic, Jon Anderson, Jayce Russell, Alex Ledford, Joshua Folmar, the sky, Patrick Yagow, NH homies, Maine homies, Nat Baldwin, Mekeel McBride, David Blair, the underground, Jon Anderson, Freddy La Force and all of Vegetarian Alcoholic Press, Godspeed! You Black Emperor, Neil Young, CAN, Dock Boggs, Andrei Tarkovsky, Mike Santora, the UNH writing community, Marc Paltrineri, Kathleen Maris Paltrineri, Claire McHenry, Ryan Harrison, Jon Vesey, Mike "Jo" Riello, Bill Stratton, and Jayme Fitzsimmons, Jonesport, Agnes, and Sophie.

Thank you, Amy Sauber, for believing in this book and in my poems, leading me onwards and upwards, and for your friendship.

None of these poems could exist, literally and spiritually without you, Mom and Dad. Thank you for encouraging me to explore the forest and be a goofball.

My deepest gratitude, love, and bow to fellow Son of Jon, and Sluggo of the Soulful Solid, David Rivard—The story is true!

Noah Burton was born in Kansas City, Kansas, in 1988. He grew up in Virginia, holds an MFA in poetry from the University of New Hampshire, and lives in Maine.

www.ingramcontent.com/pod-product-compliance
Lightning Source LLC
Chambersburg PA
CBHW032051290426
44110CB00012B/1040